*How the Stars
Get in Your Bones*

ALSO BY JAN RICHARDSON

Sparrow
The Cure for Sorrow
Circle of Grace
Through the Advent Door
In the Sanctuary of Women
In Wisdom's Path
Night Visions
Sacred Journeys

HOW THE STARS GET IN YOUR BONES

A Book *of* Blessings

JAN RICHARDSON

Wanton Gospeller Press

COPYRIGHT © 2025 BY JAN RICHARDSON
WANTON GOSPELLER PRESS

All rights reserved. Permission is granted for one-time reproduction of individual blessings for worship and educational purposes, provided that the following credit line is included: "© Jan Richardson from *How the Stars Get in Your Bones: A Book of Blessings*. janrichardson.com."

"Table Blessing," "The Midwife's Prayer," and "Benedictus" appeared in *In Wisdom's Path: Discovering the Sacred in Every Season* by Jan Richardson. Copyright © Jan Richardson.

Cover art: *Where the Light Begins*
© Jan Richardson

ISBN: 978-1-7351612-2-8

janrichardson.com wantongospeller.com

FOR DANIEL

Home

Contents

PREFACE   XI

INVITATION   XIII

AND THE TABLE WILL BE WIDE
Blessings of Welcome

    Mercy House 3
    Blessing the Threshold 5
    The Year as a House 7
    Blessing With Many Rooms 9
    And the Table Will Be Wide 11
    Table Blessing 13
    On That Night 15
    Blessing That Opens Its Heart to You 16
    Blessing That Meets You in Love 18
    The Midwife's Prayer 21
    About the Light 23
    Those Stars That Turn in Us 25
    Constellation 26
    For the Gifts That Have Come Home 28
    Blessing of Rest 30
    Blessing for Dreaming 32
    All Hallows Blessing 34

WHAT THE NIGHT IS FOR
Blessings of Healing

    What the Night Is For 39
    This Love 41
    If Perhaps the Light 42
    Every Bright Thing 44
    Blessing That Knows 45
    Remedy for Certainty 47
    Note Made of Night 48
    Blessing in Fear 49
    Blessing for Long Illness 52
    Blessing in the Storm 55
    Luminous Heart 56
    Praise Poem for the Heart 57
    Hidden Lantern 58
    Sometimes 59
    Blessing of Longing 60
    Blessing the Story 62
    Unfinished Blessing 64
    Tenderness 65
    Mending Blessing 66
    How the Stars Get in Your Bones 67
    On the Anniversary of His Death,
        She Sings of the Light by Which
        He First Arrived 70
    Say the Light 72
    Singing to the Night 74
    All This Time, Joy 76
    What Abides, What Returns 77
    Sometimes What Goes From Us 80
    Carrying the Song 81

WITNESS OF THAT LIGHT
Blessings of Sending

> Blessing to Open the Heart 85
> Blessing on a Strange Road 87
> Gabriel's Annunciation 89
> Blessing at the Burning Bush 92
> Witness of That Light 95
> For Such a Time as This 96
> This Day We Say Grateful 99
> Blessing of Elijah 102
> Blessing the Nets 104
> A Blessing With Roots 106
> Still 109
> Love Is the Most Ancient Law 112
> Saturday Morning, 10 a.m. 114
> Blessing the End of the Road 116
> Blessing the Animals 118
> Blessing the Mothers 120
> Blessing the Wedding 122
> Every Given Light 124
> Benedictus 126
> The Map Our Dreaming Makes 127

GRATITUDE 129

Preface

I try to find a place of beginning, a word by which to start. What comes instead is a pulse, the sound and rhythm of a heartbeat that moves through every blessing in this book.

I have an enduring fascination with blessings. An ancient literary form that appears across spiritual traditions, a blessing is a distinctive, sometimes poetic constellation of words designed to call upon and convey God's deep desire for our wholeness, both individually and in community. A blessing, in fact, has difficulty separating the two. Whether it appears in the formality of liturgy or in the spontaneity of daily life, a blessing arises from and depends on relationship, the connections that hold us together.

In English, the word *bless* comes from the far older word *blōd*. Referring to the use of blood in ritual acts of consecration, the word also evokes how a blessing has a kind of flow, a current on which it travels. It moves both within us and beyond us, something to be passed along rather than kept only for ourselves.

In our own time, the word *blessing* has sometimes come to connote a reward to be hoarded, a way of calculating the measure of God's benevolence toward us in the form of prosperity. The biblical understanding runs deeply counter to this. Rather than being proof of God's special favor, a blessing tends to be at its most powerful in the places of our greatest pain, fear, and loss, when the presence and love of God may be difficult to perceive.

A blessing has the ability to enter into our pain, not to dismiss or gloss over it but to name it, and to name also the love that connects us and holds us: the love that is continually working for our wholeheartedness.

In these pages, the lines of each blessing may seem straight, but the paths by which they have come—and the paths they invite us to enter—are not. Like the blood that pulses through us, these blessings move by circulation: from the heart and back to it, never returning precisely the same.

—Jan Richardson

Invitation

As I worked with the blessings Jan gathered for this collection, I began to sense a story that moves through them. Even as each blessing stands on its own, a world within itself, taken together they cast a narrative arc: the story of a soul experiencing transformation and renewal.

Here, at Jan's invitation, I share with you the journey that I find connecting the blessings across the pages of this new book.

Blessings of Welcome

The first section tells a story that I envision unfolding in one full day. A singular soul arrives outside a house, weary and disoriented and standing on the far side of the street. They face the house and know it offers an invitation to come in.

The first few blessings speak of how the house has been waiting for this soul's arrival (Mercy House, Blessing the Threshold, The Year as a House). The soul makes the decision to go inside and starts to get settled in the space (Blessing With Many Rooms).

Then comes a gathering that brings together all who have arrived at the house for their different reasons. The soul gets to know the ethos of this house and the invitation to be part of what happens there (And the Table Will Be Wide, Table Blessing). They struggle, though, to receive the invitation to stay, and they need to discern whether they will (On That Night). As they accept the invitation, the soul receives even more lavish care (Blessing That Opens Its Heart to You, Blessing That Meets You in Love). The soul is given permission to enter in fully and hold nothing back (The Midwife's Prayer).

Still seated at the table, the soul learns what it means to be part of the collective of souls who have gathered in this house (About the Light, Those Stars That Turn in Us), along with their own beautiful place in the group (Constellation). The group, together, gives thanks for the gifts that have arrived in that place (For the Gifts That Have Come Home).

Then it is time to rest. Time to let oneself fall into sweet, safe slumber and receive the healing of sleep and dreams (Blessing of Rest, Blessing for Dreaming, All Hallows Blessing).

Blessings of Healing

The second section opens with the reality of what this soul has come to the house to do, which is heal. We pick up right where the last section left off, in the nighttime, and find an invitation to let the healing be what it needs to be, without the need to control it (What the

Night Is For). In the dark, both literal and figurative, there is love (This Love). We are reminded the light is still here (If Perhaps the Light).

The blessings begin to tell of healing. Hope lies ahead, but we begin where we are (Every Bright Thing). The soul learns they are themselves a blessing, even in their disorientation (Blessing That Knows). They are encouraged to set down certainty (Remedy for Certainty) and, again, anything they still want to hold (Note Made of Night). They are greeted by whatever wants to arise and whatever is true of their experience (Blessing in Fear, Blessing for Long Illness). No matter what comes, they are assured they are not alone (Blessing in the Storm).

In all that is true and hard, the soul's heart shimmers and is strong (Luminous Heart, Praise Poem for the Heart). They are encouraged to keep going in what has begun, trusting that gifts will come (Hidden Lantern, Sometimes). It is a long road, not quickly solved; in some ways, they did not even know how much they had been needing this (Blessing of Longing). But something is happening that they cannot see or even explain (Blessing the Story). The mending and repair have begun to do their work as the soul has given themself to all of this (Unfinished Blessing, Tenderness, Mending Blessing).

This, dear one, is how the stars have been getting in your bones (How the Stars Get in Your Bones). I view this blessing—the titular one—as the inflection point in the healing section. From here, the healing still has work to do, but annunciation has come (On the Anniversary of His Death, She Sings of the Light by

Invitation

Which He First Arrived). The darkness has been long, but light has begun to arrive in a more visible way (Say the Light, Singing to the Night). With it comes the joy that had sometimes been difficult to receive (All This Time, Joy).

Then: a moment of equanimity, an ability to sit with what is and has been, and even to share the comfort of companionship with others who know this path (What Abides, What Returns). The soul is surprised by the unexpected return of gifts (Sometimes What Goes From Us) and the beginning of a song (Carrying the Song).

Blessings of Sending

I love the way the final section starts with a blessing that arrives at a door. We have traveled with the soul into the house and through a time of hospitality and healing, and now a blessing comes to ask the soul to open not just the door but also their heart (Blessing to Open the Heart). This blessing has navigated its own circuitous path (Blessing on a Strange Road) so that it might reach this door in this moment.

Then begins a series of blessings that speak to the invitation to leave the house and the soul's yes of readiness (Gabriel's Annunciation, Blessing at the Burning Bush, Witness of That Light). A blessing for departure comes (For Such a Time as This), and with it a sense of release (This Day We Say Grateful). The soul sets out from the house into their future, knowing they do so as a continuation of lineage and legacy (Blessing of

Elijah). They know also that this house is a place they can return to at any time, whenever they need what it offers.

We enter into a series of blessings that describe the road as the soul begins to walk it (Blessing the Nets, A Blessing With Roots). The soul takes with them what has been gleaned and gained from all that has happened (Still), along with the surety of who they are and what they value (Love Is the Most Ancient Law, Saturday Morning, 10 a.m.). They learn what to do when nothing is clear (Blessing the End of the Road).

Transformed by their journey, the soul returns to the world. They are no longer only a recipient of blessings but, having become a blessing, are able to share blessings with others (Blessing the Animals, Blessing the Mothers, Blessing the Wedding). In this, grace abounds (Every Given Light), a grace that meets us both this day and at the end of our days (Benedictus).

As the book closes, Jan offers us a blessing that holds both hope and light (The Map Our Dreaming Makes). Born of a deep knowing of how our path unfolds so often by unforeseen turns, this blessing gives us a glimpse of the wholeness that waits for us even as it travels with us in every moment.

—Christianne Squires, Editor

AND THE TABLE WILL BE WIDE

―――――――

Blessings of Welcome

MERCY HOUSE

You had traveled
toward it
for so long,
hardly knowing
where you were going
or that this was where
you were bound.

But when you saw it,
you knew it
for what it was,
as if you had
remembered it
into being.

There was no mistaking
the door with no lock,
the worn steps,
the wide windows
with their trick
of seeming to
look out at you
in welcome.

You return their gaze
and can sense
more than see
all who have ever
found their way here,

all who have
been gathered in
and who linger
not as ghosts
but with the sheer force
of their joy.

You know that inside,
there will be bread.
Inside, there will be wine.
There will be time enough
and rest.

And while you stand
across the street
in your hesitation,
stricken and full of longing,
in the house
built of mercy,
they will go on
quietly making ready
for you
and waiting
for as long
as it takes.

BLESSING THE THRESHOLD

This blessing
has been waiting for you
for a long time.

While you have been
making your way here,
this blessing has been
gathering itself,
making ready,
biding its time,
praying.

This blessing has been
polishing the door,
oiling the hinges,
sweeping the steps,
lighting candles
in the windows.

This blessing has been
setting the table
as it hums a tune
from an old song
it knows,
something about
a spiraling road
and bread
and grace.

All this time
it has kept an eye
on the horizon,
watching,
keeping vigil,
hardly aware of how
it was leaning itself
in your direction.

And now that
you are here,
this blessing
can hardly believe
its good fortune
that you have finally arrived,
that it can drop everything at last
to fling its arms wide
to you, crying
welcome,
welcome,
welcome.

THE YEAR AS A HOUSE

Think of the year
as a house:
door flung wide
in welcome,
threshold swept
and waiting,
a graced spaciousness
opening and offering itself
to you.

Let it be blessed
in every room.
Let it be hallowed
in every corner.
Let every nook
be a refuge
and every object
set to holy use.

Let it be here
that safety will rest.
Let it be here
that health will make its home.
Let it be here
that peace will show its face.
Let it be here
that love will find its way.

Here
let the weary come,

let the aching come,
let the lost come,
let the sorrowing come.

Here
let them find their rest,
and let them find their soothing,
and let them find their place,
and let them find their delight.

And may it be
in this house of a year
that the seasons will spin in beauty.
And may it be
in these turning days
that time will spiral with joy.
And may it be
that its rooms will fill
with ordinary grace
and light spill from every window
to welcome the stranger home.

BLESSING WITH MANY ROOMS

As you step inside
this blessing,
we wish to tell you
it is large enough
for you to lie down in.

Or (though it may not look it,
small as it is upon this page)
you can curl up
in this blessing
with a cup of tea
and a good book
beside the window—
here, just behind you—
that faces east.

Likewise it is true,
though you might not have
paused long enough
to notice,
that this blessing
is big enough
for a table—
quite a sizeable one
can be accommodated—
where your guests
will want to linger
far into the night.

And if they desire to stay,
you will find that
through this door—
you did not see it before?—
there are rooms in plenty
where they can
lay their heads
and stretch out with abandon
in their dreaming sleep.

One room,
many rooms—
in this blessing
it is all the same.

The point is that
there is space
enough:

enough to make
a life, a home;
enough to make
a world;
enough to make
your way toward
the One who has made
this way for you.

AND THE TABLE WILL BE WIDE

And the table
will be wide.
And the welcome
will be wide.
And the arms
will open wide
to gather us in.
And our hearts
will open wide
to receive.

And we will come
as children who trust
there is enough.
And we will come
unhindered and free.
And our aching
will be met
with bread.
And our sorrow
will be met
with wine.

And we will open our hands
to the feast
without shame.
And we will turn
toward each other
without fear.

And we will give up
our appetite
for despair.
And we will taste
and know
of delight.

And we will become bread
for a hungering world.
And we will become drink
for those who thirst.
And the blessed
will become the blessing.
And everywhere
will be the feast.

TABLE BLESSING

To your table
you bid us come.
You have set the places;
you have poured the wine;
and there is always room,
you say,
for one more.

And so we come.
From the streets
and from the alleys
we come.

From the deserts
and from the hills
we come.

From the ravages of poverty
and from the palaces of privilege
we come.

Running,
limping,
carried,
we come.

We are bloodied with our wars;
we are wearied with our wounds;

we carry our dead within us,
and we reckon with their ghosts.

We hold the seeds of healing;
we dream of a new creation;
we know the things
that make for peace,
and we struggle
to give them wings.

And yet, to your table
we come.
Hungering for your bread,
we come;
thirsting for your wine,
we come;
singing your song
in every language,
speaking your name
in every tongue,
in conflict and in communion,
in discord and in desire,
we come,
O God of Wisdom,
we come.

ON THAT NIGHT

On that night when
you are holding
your very last hope,
thinking to let it go
as too small to be saved
or sanctified;

on that night when
you turn away at last
from the far horizon
over which you had thought
your life would come
to find you;

on that night,
believe me,
this is where
the ache
will give way
to the mystery

and the blessing
that seemed so distant
will quietly
come to meet you,

holding your heart
in its two
luminous hands.

Blessings of Welcome

BLESSING THAT OPENS ITS HEART TO YOU

You have seen
the impostors
trying to masquerade
as this blessing,
how they cloak themselves
with words
that look so much
like what you longed for,
while beneath
they are hollow.

This blessing
has come to tell you:
do not be discouraged,
do not be dismayed,
do not berate yourself
for where you have been
searching,
for the wisdom that comes
along what seems
a foolish road.

You will know this blessing
by how it opens its heart
to you.
You will know this blessing
by how it turns its face
toward you.

You will know this blessing
by how it approaches you
arm in arm with faith
and hope.

You will know this blessing
not by the ease it offers you
but by what it asks of you:
patience and kindness,
forbearance and belief,
hope and endurance,
and more,

not because this is what
you owe
but because this is what
this blessing stirs in you,
what it provides for you,
what it pours into your hands
that you suddenly
find open,

like your heart
that unfolds itself
in welcome,
finally knowing
and fully known.

Blessings of Welcome

BLESSING THAT MEETS YOU IN LOVE

It is true that
every blessing begins
with love,
that whatever else
it might say,
love is always
precisely its point.

But it should be noted
that this blessing
has come today
especially to tell you
it is crazy about you.
That it has been
in love with you
forever.
That it has never
not wanted
to see your face,
to go through this world
in your company.

This blessing thought
it was high time
it told you so,
just to make sure
you know.

If it has been shy
in saying this,
it has not been
for any lack of
wanting to.
It's just that
this blessing
knows the risk
of offering itself
in a way that
will so alter you—
because this is
simply where
loving leads.

This blessing knows
how love undoes us,
unhinges us,
unhides us.

It knows
how loving
can sometimes feel
like dying.

But today
this blessing
has come to tell you
the secret

Blessings of Welcome

that sends it
to your door:
that it gives itself
to those
willing to come alive;
that it vows itself
to those
ready to be
born anew.

THE MIDWIFE'S PRAYER

Keep screaming, little baby girl.
Keep practicing using those lungs
and do not stop,
because hollering will help
to ease the shock
every time you go through
another birth.

Practice squalling
so that your voice is clear and strong
when you speak,
and when your breath
has been knocked from you,
practice breathing small,
but do not stop.

There are miles
of blood vessels in those lungs;
use every inch,
and know the voices
that run in those veins,
the voices that fill your breath,
that will inhabit
your words when you speak
and your groans when you weep
and your mouth when you laugh
and your cries in nights of wild love
and your whispers when you pray.

Blessings of Welcome

So keep screaming, little baby girl,
not for that warm, dark place you lost,
but for all the darkness
you will find inside you
that will need to be spoken
with words only you can say.

ABOUT THE LIGHT

As of yet
I cannot say
which I love best
about the light:

that it gathers itself
even in what goes hidden,
no stranger to
the seed, the stone,
the labyrinth of night,

or that it is wildly
generous in where
it lands, glad the same
to touch the face of
the one in laughter,
the one in tears,
the one in trouble,
in fear, in pain.

But it may yet be
that this is what
enchants me most
about the light:

that it knows
what to do with distance,
how it arcs
across the space

Blessings of Welcome

between a heart
and a heart,
illuminating the longing
through which
the farthest of stars
might be seen.

THOSE STARS THAT TURN IN US

I do not know
how to keep it all together
or by what patterns
this world might
finally hold.

What I know is
our hearts are bigger
than this sky
that wheels above us

and what shines
through all this darkness
shines through us,
setting every shattered thing
into a new constellation,

and we can turn
our faces
to that light,
to the grace of
those stars
that turn in us.

CONSTELLATION

Consider that the heart
holds its own constellation.

Consider that it has
a secret chamber
radiant with unspent light.

Consider this when you cannot find
that one star, that dream
that compels you to the road.

When every last thing seems
to have disappeared into dark,
consider that you cannot always know
how you bear this brightness
but that it holds you
and is not wasted
or lost.

See how we share this sky,
how it stretches above us
beyond every border,
how every day
turns each of us
in steady revolution
through morning, night,
morning again.

Or think of it like this:
that every heart is its own harbor,
sending its vessels out,
drawing them back again,
never by the same way they went
but still somehow making for
home, that place that shimmers
now in welcome
with all the gathered light
you had thought
you could not see.

FOR THE GIFTS THAT HAVE COME HOME

Praise
for this day.
Praise
for the paths
that have carried
us here.
Praise
for the hands
that have made
a way,
for the hearts
that have opened,
for the gifts
that have come
home.

Praise for this hour
when we choose to say
we see you,
when we rejoice to say
we recognize you,
when we dare to say
we call you
here,
we welcome you
here,
we bless you
here.

Praise for this moment
when we stand
with you.
Praise for this threshold
that opens
to us.
Praise for the mystery
that makes itself known
in vision, in dream,
in prayer, in grace,
in the love
that has led us
and called us
by name.

Blessings of Welcome

BLESSING OF REST

Curl this blessing
beneath your head
for a pillow.
Wrap it about yourself
for a blanket.
Lay it across your eyes
and for this moment,
cease thinking about
what comes next,
what you will do
when you rise.

Let this blessing
gather itself to you
like the stillness
that descends
between your heartbeats,
the silence that comes
so briefly
but with a constancy
on which
your life depends.

Settle yourself
into the quiet
this blessing brings,
the hand it lays
upon your brow,

the whispered word
it breathes into
your ear,
telling you
all shall be well,
and all shall be well,
and you can rest
now.

BLESSING FOR DREAMING

This blessing begins
behind your eyelids
when at last
you close them
for sleep,
and all that you have seen
in this day
begins to play itself
again.

You watch the scenes
as they repeat themselves:
everything done
or undone,
all the moments that brought
worry or delight,
the meetings and crossings
that gave gladness
or pain.

Let these scenes unwind,
and then
let them go.

Beneath them,
behind them,
other pictures wait,
wanting to draw your gaze,

like paintings
on the walls of a chapel
no one has seen
for centuries
or shimmering from the pages
of an ancient prayer book
that falls open
in your hands.

Open the eyes
behind your eyes
and see what reveals itself
only in the dark,
only in this house
made of dreaming,
where you can
lay yourself down
in peace.

ALL HALLOWS BLESSING

Who live
in the spaces between
our breathing

in the corner
of our vision

in the hollows
of our bones

in the chambers
of our heart:

nowhere can they
be touched
yet still

how they move us

how they move
in us

made from the
tissue of memory
like the veil
between the worlds

that stirs at
the merest breath
this night
and then is
at rest.

WHAT THE NIGHT IS FOR

―――――――――

Blessings of Healing

WHAT THE NIGHT IS FOR

Oh my heart,
if we could cease working
on our sorrow
like we were trying
to stitch together
shattered glass.

This breaking
is not for fixing,
as though
if we could just find
the fitting tool,
everything would tumble
into its place,
joined and whole.

Perhaps it is time
to let the shards lie
where they have fallen.

Perhaps it is time
to let ourselves
sit and weep
over them.

And then perhaps
we scatter them—
into the soil,
into the sky,

Blessings of Healing

it does not matter
where.

Let them take
their place.
Let them shimmer
like a constellation
in all that darkness—

sky-dark, soil-dark,
at home in that strange
and radiant solace
that knows
what the night
is for,

how it takes
the broken things
and sets them
shining
to light our way
from here.

THIS LOVE

When the night
has come
and the dark.

When the questions
wrap us round
and the wondering.

When you speak to us
what we can hardly fathom
or absorb.

Then let it come
like a heartbeat,
like a breath—

this love,
this love,
this love.

IF PERHAPS THE LIGHT

If we thought the light
was done.

If we thought the gift of it
had gone.

If we thought it had turned
its grace from us,
spent by our resistance,
undone by distance
and time.

But if perhaps
we wait.

If perhaps
we turn and
watch.

If perhaps
we let ourselves breathe
at last
in receiving and
release—
*one, two, three,
a million.*

If perhaps
we learn
that the light knows
how to bend,
how to endure
long after first given,
how to circle back
in generous, luminous
return.

If perhaps
the light does not
end.

Blessings of Healing

EVERY BRIGHT THING

If I could write this blessing
backward,
I would begin it
at the end.

I would start it
from that far place where
I could show you
every bright thing
that lies ahead for you,
radiant in its wholeness
and complete
in its own joy.

For now,
all I can offer
is this blessing that
begins here—
in the gap,
in the hollow,
in the hope
that tells us

this is how a blessing
becomes;
this is how a blessing
is made:
from the broken things
we travel with
from here.

BLESSING THAT KNOWS

This blessing
has been aching
with a heart
broken
and lost
and tired.

It does not have it
all together.
It sometimes wakes up
anxious and afraid.

This blessing
had to be quiet,
had to let itself sit
in stillness and sorrow,
had to let itself stop and rest.

This blessing knows
you carry your own sorrow,
your own grief.
It knows the weariness
that visits you,
the questions
that attend your road.

It knows, too,
how you keep turning yourself
toward mystery,

keep turning yourself
toward hope,
keep turning yourself
toward this world
with the beautiful stubbornness
by which a way
is made.

And so this blessing is glad
to cross your path,
to see your face,
to speak your name,
to offer thanks.

It meets you
with glad welcome
and fierce love
both ancient
and present.

This blessing
comes to you
with heart impossibly open
for the blessing
that you bear,
the blessing
that you are.

REMEDY FOR CERTAINTY

It can seem like
small comfort,
I know,
to let it go,
to release our hold
on the certainty
whose precision
we have counted on
all this time,
that blade
with which
we have cut through
every doubt.

When mystery
comes, then,
may we open
our hands.

May we give ourselves
into the uneasy mercy
that meets us with
its curious remedy

and the healing
a question
can hold.

Blessings of Healing

NOTE MADE OF NIGHT

Let it fall apart.

Let it fall apart
some more,

the blessing of it
worn beyond
all recognizing

but strangely whole
as it finds its way
to you,

every edge of it
a threshold

and you can enter
anywhere.

BLESSING IN FEAR

Raw in every nerve—
without rest,
without trust,
without hope,
and, it seems,
without grace.

The ache
in your heart,
the hollow
in your gut,
the grind
in your jaw
bear witness
to how long
you have been without
peace.

You think
if you could just
take one deep breath,
if you could still
the clamor
and the chaos
for just one moment,
you could feel again
the ground
beneath your feet,

Blessings of Healing

could find your way back
to what once held you
to this earth.

This blessing
will not try
to explain away
your fear.

It will not tell you
you should not feel
the fear.

It will not say to you
that love casts out
all fear.

It will not try
to persuade you
not to fear.

This blessing knows
in this world
there is good cause
to be afraid,
so it will not appeal
to your reason.

Instead, it will go straight
for your heart,
breathe itself
into every chamber,
travel every
frightened nerve.

It may be quiet
in the ways
it works its soothing.

Let it be enough to know
it is there,
bearing itself
into your blood,
humming its song
through every vein,
claiming every cell of you
for courage
and for peace.

BLESSING FOR LONG ILLNESS

There is nothing this blessing
would like more than
to lay itself down
beside you,
to wrap its arms
around you
in your deepest weariness,
your sharpest pain.

This blessing knows the hope
you carry
and the hopelessness
you sometimes feel.

It sees the courage
that illumines you
and the shadows
that attend your days.

This blessing breathes
through those who want to help
but who cannot know
how it feels
to inhabit your flesh
that has been so long
examined and invaded
or how your heart gives way

each time the things
that come to heal
bring their own poison
and pain.

This blessing knows
you want to make this
easier for others,
let alone for yourself,
that you want
for all
and all
to be well.

This blessing hardly
knows what to say,
but it will meet you
in every weariness.

It will come to you
in every pain.

It will stay with you
in every hope found
and lost
and found again.

It will keep making
its way to you

Blessings of Healing

with fierce grace
and stubborn love,
those twin medicines borne
in both its hands.

BLESSING IN THE STORM

This blessing cannot claim
to still the storm
that has seized you,
cannot calm
the waves that wash
through your soul,
that break against
your fierce and
aching heart.

But it will wade
into these waters,
will stand with you
in this storm,
will say *peace* to you
in the waves,
peace to you
in the winds,
peace to you
in every moment
that finds you still
within the storm.

Blessings of Healing

LUMINOUS HEART

When the lines
of your life
fall heavy and dark,

when the layers
lie tangled and frayed
and every story
seems a scar
written sore
upon you,

then may you
know yourself
held in that light
that gives every line
back to you,

inscribed in the love
that has always
been traced across
your luminous heart.

PRAISE POEM FOR THE HEART

Praise for the heart
persistent in its beating,
beautiful in its enduring,
wondrous as it holds

through the fracture,
through the rupture,
through the breaking—

how it goes on
in hopeful cadence,
in every chamber
whole.

Blessings of Healing

HIDDEN LANTERN

Steady, love;
this is what
the struggle
is for,

the press
of darkness
and time
making its own light,

as if in the earth
a hidden lantern
or in the seed
a star

that blossoms finally
into the yielding night,
bearing forth
the radiant day.

SOMETIMES

Sometimes
give in.

Sometimes
give way.

Sometimes
give up,
give out.

Sometimes
give ground.

Sometimes
crumble into
the grace
that enters
the remnant,
the ruin.

Sometimes
fall into
the love
that sees
how to begin again,
again.

BLESSING OF LONGING

You hardly knew
how parched
it was possible
to become.

You did not ask
for this desert,
did not seek
the thirst
that now inhabits
every moment
of every day.

You would not
have guessed
how this blessing
is written within
your wanting,

how each line of it
lives inside
your longing.

But listen
and it will tell you
where the wellsprings
lie within
this weary land.

Look
and it will show you
how to cup your hands
for the water
whose worth
you never knew
till now.

BLESSING THE STORY

You might think
this blessing lives
in the story
you can see,
that it has curled up
in a comfortable spot
on the surface
of the telling.

But this blessing lives
in the story beneath
the story.
It lives in the story
inside the story,
in the spaces between,
in the edges,
the margins,
the mysterious gaps,
the enticing and
fertile emptiness.

This blessing
makes its home
within the layers.
It is doorway and portal,
passage and path.
It is more ancient
than imagining

and creates itself
ever new.

This blessing
is where the story
begins again.

UNFINISHED BLESSING

I have
only the beginning
of this blessing,
only the first words
of what it might
become—

this, and
a wild trust
in the beauty
that meets us
unfinished
and the grace
that lives
at the edge,

where joy
pieces itself together
and delight
comes frayed
and glorious

and where you hold
the words that
happen next
in this prayer
that does not end.

TENDERNESS

If it breaks
our heart,
no matter;
the tenderness
that undoes us
knows also
how to mend,

like the needle
that stitches up
the willing cloth,
piercing as it
repairs.

MENDING BLESSING

Oh my friend,
take heart.
The work of repair
is aching
in its slowness
and beautiful in
the inches by which
it will arrive.

Do not pray to be patient
but to persist.
Ask for the endurance
that helps us learn
to breathe
in the midst of fear,
to love
in the presence
of sorrow,
to dream
within the rending
of the world that might
be made.

HOW THE STARS GET IN YOUR BONES

Sapphire, diamond, emerald, quartz:
think of every hard thing
that carries its own brilliance,
shining with the luster that comes
only from uncountable ages
in the earth, in the dark,
buried beneath unimaginable weight,
bearing what seemed impossible,
bearing it still.

And you, shouldering the grief
you had thought so solid, so impermeable,
the terrible anguish
you carried as a burden
now become—
who can say what day it happened?—
a beginning.

See how the sorrow in you
slowly makes its own light,
how it conjures its own fire.

See how radiant
even your despair has become
in the grace of that sun.

Did you think this would happen
by holding the weight of the world,

Blessings of Healing

by giving in to the press of sadness
and time?

I tell you, this blazing in you—
it does not come by choosing
the most difficult way, the most daunting;
it does not come by the sheer force
of your will.
It comes from the helpless place in you
that, despite all, cannot help but hope,
the part of you that does not know
how not to keep turning
toward this world,
to keep turning your face
toward this sky,
to keep turning your heart
toward this unendurable earth,
knowing your heart will break
but turning it still.

I tell you,
this is how the stars
get in your bones.

This is how the brightness
makes a home in you,
as you open to the hope that burnishes
every fractured thing it finds
and sets it shimmering,

a generous light that will not cease,
no matter how deep the darkness grows,
no matter how long the night becomes.

Still, still, still,
the secret of secrets
keeps turning in you,
becoming beautiful,
becoming blessed,
kindling the luminous way
by which you will emerge,
carrying your shattered heart
like a constellation within you,
singing to the day
that will not fail to come.

ON THE ANNIVERSARY OF HIS DEATH, SHE SINGS OF THE LIGHT BY WHICH HE FIRST ARRIVED

Let it be said you arrived
like an annunciation that night,
a tangle of light and song,
ghost of wing promising
equal parts shelter
and flight.

No angel, you, but you knew
about the weak points between worlds,
those membranes that give way
to the strange meetings
it takes a strong heart
to hold.

You lived betwixt.

So, sure, I can see you kin
to that herald who came hailing
the girl who had been minding
her own self until the moment
he alighted, a luminous tumble
of flesh and wing and word, saying
blessed are you and
do not fear and
you will bear.

Imagine the blazing of
that moment, the brilliance
not even visible, perhaps, but
seared into her bones
by the collision of speech and fire
that would send her from there
quickened and
marked.

You entered like that.

More subtle, perhaps,
but with unmistakable heat
and a cadence not entirely
of this earth.

And blessed am I
who bear it now:
scar of what burned between us,
testimony to that fearsome,
gladsome light that struck
like a match to the heart,
radiating into a map
beneath my skin,
the lines of it singing
as they show the way
from here.

SAY THE LIGHT

Say the night
was long.

Say the angels
kept vigil,
and the creatures;
that the stars stood still
in their course.

Say even the shadows
held their breath,
stretched toward what
they could not see,
lending it their hiddenness
to shelter it from view.

Say at the darkest hour
the day broke
into astonished wonder,
that it arrived first as song,
then as flesh,
then as love
radiant in its joy.

Say the light lives.

Say it will never spend itself,
that it is stubborn,
that it endures.

Say the light
is what we hold
for each other,
carrying it in the marrow,
the hollow of the heart
that splinters open in hope
to illumine
every shattered thing.

SINGING TO THE NIGHT

Who would have thought
the sky could be so pierced
or that it could pour forth such
light through the breach
whose shape matched
so precisely
the hole in the heart
that had ached
for long ages,
weary from all its emptying?

And what had once been
a wound
opened now,
like a door
or a dream,
radiant in its welcome,
singing to the night
that would prove itself
at last
not endless.

Call the piercing a star.
Call it the place the light begins.
Call it the point that tethers us
to this sheltering sky.

Call it the hope
that keeps holding us

74 *How the Stars Get in Your Bones*

to this broken,
blessed earth,
that keeps turning us
toward this world,
luminous beneath
its shadows.

Call it the vigil fire
kept in that place
where every last thing
will be mended
and we will see one another
finally whole,
shining like
the noonday sun.

ALL THIS TIME, JOY

In all this dark,
did you think
joy had forgotten you,
as if you could have
merely slipped its mind
while it absconded
to sit by some other fire?

When all this time,
joy has been
singing your name
to the stars
that have never ceased
to shine.

WHAT ABIDES, WHAT RETURNS

In a season of stunning sun,
we have chosen the only day
of rain,
and so we shelter on this porch,
each with a cup in hand
and in our heart a hole
in the precise shape
of our beloved.

I have not come here
to compare notes,
widow to widow,
that untimely word
still harsh in my ear,

but simply
to sit together
in the stillness
at the edge of that wound,
the sound of our voices
a testament
to what endures,
to the unbearable
somehow borne.

Easter draws near
as we watch the rain.
We know the drama
and the pageantry

Blessings of Healing

that lie ahead,
the commotion that is owed
such a miracle.

Meanwhile, we go on
quietly raising the dead,
tending them as more
than a memory,
learning to live in
the curious marriage
of absence and presence
that settles into the bones
and the aching
but durable heart.

We know resurrection as something
not merely to be anticipated
but also daily lived
as we reckon with
what abides,
what returns
of the beloved
who cannot be unknown—
who, having passed into us,
will not be so easily shed.

Still, I think of Mary Magdalene
and the secret she carried

when she left
that empty tomb:
how resurrection is
a strange dance
of reunion and release;
how our loving
will always ask of us
a letting go,

yet in the asking
a promise
that what we love
knows how to find us,
even by the path
that will bear us
far away
from here.

SOMETIMES WHAT GOES FROM US

Perhaps it will come
as the lightest thing
imaginable,
a gentleness
you had thought
impossible,
nesting in the hollow
of your hand,

the blessed
gift of it
nothing you would
have dreamed
but for how it now
appears,
come to tell you

sometimes
what goes from us,
remains;

sometimes
what flies from us,
returns.

CARRYING THE SONG

Call it everything
that travels
on the current
that moves between us,
where what had been
unsayable
becomes, somehow,
said

and all that lay
in silence
finds its cadence,
finds its flow,
finds the edge
of its own voice
and cannot help
but sing.

WITNESS OF THAT LIGHT

―――――

Blessings of Sending

BLESSING TO OPEN THE HEART

It may astonish you
how quietly this blessing
arrives.

No hammering
at the door.
No chiming
of the bell.

It has given
no warning,
sent no message
in advance,

yet with a suddenness
that somehow comes
as no surprise,
it is there
on the doorstep
of your heart.

Peer out,
and you will see
this blessing is no stranger.
You already know
every word
it has come to say.

I am merely here
to tell you

Blessings of Sending

how this blessing
is a remembering,
a returning,
how it asks of you
what you already long
to do:

open,
open,
open.

BLESSING ON A STRANGE ROAD

If this blessing could have found you
on its own, it would have.
As it happened, it had to depend
on the mercy of other travelers
willing to bring it here.

This blessing was borne along
in other languages,
carried by cadences
not your own.

It was slipped into a pocket,
hidden in the corner of a bag,
tucked among the pages
of a book.

This blessing was exchanged
once for bread,
once for salt,
and another time for tea.

For a while it traveled
tight in the grip of a child,
crossed a border by night,
rested in the blaze of day.

Now this blessing meets you
looking like nothing you have known,

fragrant with some far scent
and humming an unfamiliar song.

Still, somehow
it calls you by your name,
curls into your hand,
settles inside your heart as if
it has always belonged.

Not for keeping,
not for keeping
has this blessing come.
You will know
when it is time
to send it on its way.

Act surprised when it reappears
long after you thought it gone.
This blessing is strange like that,
how it stays with you
even in its absence,
how it lingers after leaving
so you do not go alone.

GABRIEL'S ANNUNCIATION

For a moment
I hesitated
on the threshold.
For the space
of a breath
I paused,
unwilling to disturb
her last ordinary moment,
knowing that the next step
would cleave her life,
that this day
would slice her story
in two,
dividing all the days before
from all the ones
to come.

The artists would later
depict the scene:
Mary, dazzled
by the archangel,
her head bowed
in humble assent,
awed by the messenger
who condescended
to leave paradise
to bestow such an honor
upon a woman, and mortal.

Blessings of Sending

Yet I tell you
it was I who was dazzled,
I who found myself agape
when I came upon her—
reading, at the loom, in the kitchen,
I cannot now recall,
only that the woman before me,
blessed and full of grace
long before I called her so,
shimmered with how completely
she inhabited herself,
inhabited the space around her,
inhabited the moment
that hung between us.

I wanted to save her
from what I had been sent
to say.

Yet when the time came,
when I had stammered
the invitation
(history would not record
the sweat on my brow,
the pounding of my heart,
would not note
that I said
do not be afraid
to myself as much as

to her),
it was she
who saved me—
her first deliverance—
her *let it be*
not just declaration
to the Divine
but a word of solace,
of soothing,
of benediction

for the angel
in the doorway
who would hesitate
one last time—
just for the space
of a breath
torn from his chest—
before wrenching himself away
from her radiant consent,
her beautiful and
awful *yes*.

BLESSING AT THE BURNING BUSH

You will have to decide
if you want this—
want the blessing
that comes to you
on an ordinary day,
when you are minding
your own path,
bent on the task before you
that you have done
a hundred times,
a thousand.

You will have to choose
for yourself
whether you will attend
to the signs;
whether you will open your eyes
to the searing light, the heat;
whether you will open
your ears, your heart
to the voice
that knows your name,
that tells you this place
where you stand—
this ground so familiar
and therefore unregarded—
is, in fact,
holy.

You will have to discern
whether you have
defenses enough
to rebuff the call,
excuses sufficient
to withstand the pull
of what blazes before you;
whether you will
hide your face,
will turn away,
back toward—
what, exactly?

No path from here
could ever be
ordinary again,
could ever become
unstrange to you,
whose seeing
has been scorched
beyond all salving.

You will know your path
not by how it shines
before you
but by how it burns
within you,
leaving you whole
as you go from here,

blazing with
your inarticulate,
your inescapable
yes.

WITNESS OF THAT LIGHT

There is no telling
how it will come,
what day it will arrive—

a brightness that begins
in the bones,
a light that constellates
in the heart
while our attention
is, for a moment,
elsewhere.

When it appears,
testify.
When it shows up,
declare.

Give witness to
the unaccountable grace
that enters in
unseen

to shine forth
from every cell,
going out to
all it meets.

FOR SUCH A TIME AS THIS

for the women bishops

Oh my sisters—
you who make
a home for God
within the space
of yourself;
you who have accepted
outrageous invitations
from the hand
of the Divine;
you who have spoken
an audacious
let it be
that propels you still
onto a road
with no map,
no markers,
no compass but
a fierce and tender faith:

May you know
the blessing that you bear,
the blessing that you are,
the blessing that has been
inscribed upon you,
laid down like your life
in words
emblazoned by fire,

traced with tears,
and marked by
an aching joy.

May you see how,
like Mary,
your life sings
of a world turned right,
how your being proclaims
the hope you have carried
like a child
beneath your heart.

May you rejoice
in the sanctuary
of your sisters
present and seen
and remember
the unseen hands
that lay themselves—
still—
upon your head
in a continual blessing
and consecration,

bearing you up,
offering secret manna,

sustaining you
and sending you forth
for such a time
as this.

THIS DAY WE SAY GRATEFUL

It is a strange thing
to be so bound
and so released
all in the same moment,
to feel the heart
open wide
and wider still,
even as it turns
to take its leave.

On this day,
let us say
this is simply the way
love moves
in its ceaseless spiraling,
turning us toward
one another,
then sending us
into what waits for us
with arms open wide to us
in welcome
and in hope.

On this day,
in this place
where you have
poured yourself out,

Blessings of Sending

where you have been
emptied
and filled
and emptied again,
may you be aware
more than ever
of what your heart
has opened to
here,
what it has tended
and welcomed
here,
where it has broken
in love and in grief,
where it has given
and received blessing
in the unfathomable mystery
that moves us,
undoes us,
and remakes us,
finally,
for joy.

This day
may you know
this joy
in full measure.

This day
may you know
this blessing
that gathers you in
and sends you forth
but will not
forget you.

Oh hear us
as this day
we say
grace,
this day
we say
grateful,
this day
we say
blessing,
this day
we release you
into God's keeping
and hold you
in gladness
and love.

BLESSING OF ELIJAH

Make no mistake.
This blessing that comes
like hands laid
upon your head,
a mantle draped
across your shoulders:
you do not bear it
alone.

Think of it
as lineage,
as litany,
an ancient legacy
entwining you among the strands
that weave through
generations and centuries,
that spiral with
the enduring and
determined grace
of the story that has
seized you
and the One
who has claimed
and called you.

Take heart
that this blessing
comes to you
singed and scorched,

signed by the blazing
of wonders
you can barely imagine
and by trials
that have already tested you,
else you would not
have found your way
this far.

Lay it down
and it will be a path for you
across terrain
you never envisioned
daring to cross.

Take it up
and know the presence
of those who have passed this
on to you,
who encompass you,
who enfold you,
who go with you
and give you
to the road
that is your own,
held in the Love
that has called
your name.

BLESSING THE NETS

You could cast it
in your sleep,
its familiar arc
embedded in your
muscle memory
after months,
years,
a lifetime
of gathering in
what you had thought
would sustain you
forever.

You would not
have imagined
it would be so easy
to cast aside,
would never have believed
the immediacy
with which your hands
could release their
familiar grip,
could let it go,
could let it simply continue
its arcing path
away from you.

But when the call came,
you did not hesitate

to follow,
as if your body
had suddenly remembered
the final curve
of the arc,

as if the release
begun in your hands
now passed through you
entirely,
and you let go
of everything

to cast yourself
with abandon
into the waiting
world.

A BLESSING WITH ROOTS

Tug at this blessing
and you will find
it is a thing
with roots.

This is a blessing
that has gone deep
into good soil,
into the sacred dark,
into the luminous hidden.

It has been months
since the ground
gathered the seed
of this blessing
into itself,
years since the earth
enfolded it.

Sometimes
that's how long
a blessing takes.

And the fact
that this blessing
should finally show
its first fruits
on the day
you happened by—

well, perhaps we shall
simply call the timing
of this ripening
a mystery
and a sweet grace.

Take all you want
of this blessing.
Take every morsel
you need for
the path ahead.
Let its fruits fall
into your hands;
gather them into
the basket of
your arms.

Let this blessing
be one place
where you are willing
to receive
in unmeasured portions,
to lay aside
for a moment
the way you ration
your delights.

Let yourself accept
its inexplicable plenitude;

allow it to give itself
to sustain you,

not simply for yourself—
though on this bright day,
I might be persuaded
to think that would
be enough—

but that you may
gather its seeds
into yourself,
like the ground
where this blessing began,

and wait
with the patience
of seasons
and of years

to bear forth
in the fullness of time
a stunning harvest,
a plenteous feast.

STILL

*for my parents on their 60th anniversary,
after the hurricane*

Sweeping the walk after the storm,
I marveled at the blossoms
that remained on the bush.
They seemed a miracle,
stubborn in their enduring,
as if to say, *See?*
Beauty is not lost
so easily as you thought.

Sometimes we grow accustomed
to the pummeling life gives us,
grow used to the fierce winds
that blow us far from where
we thought to go
before tumbling us into

the eye, the eye, the eye,
where it can be most difficult
to see, not knowing whether
this is a lasting calm
or the tempest
regathering itself,
strengthening into a force
that can pull apart a life,
a world.

Blessings of Sending

What we finally learn is this:
before the storm,
within the storm,
beyond the storm,
the still point
still holds,
making possible the pivot,
the turn toward what calls
us on from here,
carrying the stillness with us.

And this is what I mean to say,
what I want for you to see:
the still point that you are,
the centered and centering calm
that creates itself again and again
from the steady graces born
of more than twenty thousand days
you have spent drawing deep
and deep from the love
that holds you,

like the seed that contains
both root and flower
in the inexplicable promise
that tells us

come wind,
come rain,

come dark
and the close,
impenetrable night,

there is shelter,
there is peace,
there is the spacious,
encompassing heart
that gives us rest
within the raging
and surprises us with blooms
beyond the storm.

LOVE IS THE MOST ANCIENT LAW

Open to it
and you will know
how love is
its own blessing
and most ancient
of laws.

Pursue it
entirely,
with everything
in you—
your heart
(all),
your soul
(all),
your mind
(all).

Spend it
all—
this love
so generous,
this love
that goes out
to each
it finds,
this love
that gives itself

in lavish and
unimagined measure
everywhere and
to all—

yourself
not least.

SATURDAY MORNING, 10 A.M.

Justice and Peace meet at the café,
sit together,
hands folded around steaming cups,
heads bent over the paper.

They are not taking in
the news of the world
with sorrowing eyes
and the clucking of tongues.

They are instead planning their itinerary,
plotting their map,
looking for the places where
they might slip in.

Their fingers touch, release,
touch again as they read,
moving with the half-aware habits
that come only with long living alongside.

They have met, parted,
met again on countless mornings
like this one, torn and taken
by turns.

They put the paper aside.
They brush away the crumbs.
They talk quietly.
They know there is work to do.

But they order one more cup;
there is savoring they must do
before the saving begins.

They lean in,
barely touching
across the table for
a kiss that makes a way,
a world.

BLESSING THE END OF THE ROAD

When you come
to the end
of the road,
the spiraling turn,
the bend beyond which
you cannot see,
may your first practice be
to breathe.

May your second practice be
to breathe again.

Keep at this.
Watch.
Wait.

See what road appears
that you did not think
a road,
what path is found
by patience,
what map is made
by taking up
the third practice:

to keep breathing,
stubborn in the rhythm
of intake and release

by which you will
fill your yearning lungs,
not for the waiting road
but for your leap
by which the road
will come.

BLESSING THE ANIMALS

You who created them
and called them good:

Bless again these creatures
who come to us
as a blessing,
fashioned of fur
or feather
or fin,
formed of flesh
that breathes with
your own breath,
that you have made
from sheer delight,
that you have given
in dazzling variety.

Bless them
who curl themselves
around our hearts,
who twine themselves
through our days,
who companion us
in our labor,
who call us
to come and play.

Bless them
who will never be
entirely tamed
and so remind us
that you love
what is wild,
that you rejoice
in what lives close
to the earth,
that your heart beats
in the heart of these creatures
you have entrusted
to our care.

BLESSING THE MOTHERS

Who are our
first sanctuary.

Who fashion
a space of blessing
with their own being:

with the belly,
the bone,
and the blood—

or,
if not with these,
then with the
durable heart
that offers itself
to break
and grow wide,
to gather itself
around another
as refuge,
as home.

Who lean into
the wonder and terror
of loving what
they can hold
but cannot contain.

Who remain
in some part of themselves
always awake,
a corner of consciousness
keeping perpetual vigil.

Who know
that a story
is what endures,
is what binds us,
is what runs deeper
even than blood,

and so they spin them
in celebration
of what abides
and benediction
on what remains:

a simple gladness
that latches on to us
and graces us
on our way.

BLESSING THE WEDDING

I will tell you,
dearly beloved,
it is clear to us
who have gathered
around you this day
that this blessing already
dances between you.

That it has already
made its home within you.

That it began
to take up residence
long ago
in the place made by
the opening of your hearts
toward one another.

This blessing
is no stranger to you,
but today let us say
we will call it
what it is—
this love,
gentle and fierce,
that takes its place
with you.

This day,
let us say
that we will welcome it
in glad measure,
that we will celebrate it
with unstinting joy,
that we will safeguard it
without reservation.

This day
and all to come,
may you see
what we see
between you;
may you know
what we know
because of you:

the blessing of love
that abides,
that gives itself
with delight,
that offers itself
with abandon,
that lays itself down
and moves us
to rise again.

EVERY GIVEN LIGHT

There are days
we think
only so much
is given—
a glint,
a gleam,
a light so small
we could carry it
in the palm of
our hand,
just enough
to let us see
the next step,
perhaps,
into the mystery.

There are days
grace comes
but in shadow,
days it gathers itself
into the corners,
days it seems
to turn its gaze
sidelong,
as if distracted
or pondering
or paused.

Let it be said
this is not
that day.

This is the day
when grace
gives out
its radiance,
declaring itself
to everything
in sight.

This is the day
when every given light
bears forth
like a star,
turning its face
toward us with
the brilliance
that was there
all along,
that it had saved
just for us,
just for the joy
of seeing us
shine.

BENEDICTUS

In your leaving,
we say peace.
With the last light of you dying,
we say peace.
And where there is no peace,
we say peace,
in the hope it will rest in our bones.

In your going,
we say joy.
With the last breath of you leaving,
we say joy.
And where there is no joy,
we say joy,
in the hope it will dwell in our flesh.

In your departing,
we say love.
With the earth taking you in,
we say love.
And where there is no love,
we say love,
in the hope it will come to our souls.

THE MAP OUR DREAMING MAKES

I cannot tell you
how far I have come
to give this blessing
to you.

No map
for the distance crossed,
no measure
for the terrain behind,
no calendar
for marking
the passage of time
while I traveled a road
I knew not.

For now, let us say
I had to come by
a different star
than the one
I first followed,
had to navigate by
another dream
than the one
I loved the most.

But I tell you
that even here,
the hope

that each star belongs
to a light
more ancient still,

and each dream
part of the way
that lies beneath
this way,

and each day
drawing us closer
to the day
when every path
will converge

and we will see the map
our dreaming made,
luminous in every line
that finally led us
home.

Gratitude

As this book came together, a great deal of life happened. I am grateful for those whose hearts have held me through it all and who are a blessing beyond measure. They include Peg Carlson-Hoffman, Chuck Hoffman, Carol Wilson, Carolyn Mathis, Dorri Sherrill, Leslee Lyndon Wray, Lesley Brogan, Karen Weatherford, Kathy Craven, Emily Wray, Brenda Lewis, Barbie Boyd, Maru Ladròn de Guevara, and Jim Knipper.

I offer particular gratitude for my beloved family: my parents, Judy and Joe; my brother and sister-in-law, Scott and Lacinda; and my sister and brother-in-law, Sally and Craig. I give thanks also for the Doles family.

My extraordinary editor and friend Christianne Squires has blessed me in both of these roles with her wisdom and heart.

I am thankful beyond words for Daniel Nevins.

And to you, deep gratitude and every blessing.

About the Author

Jan Richardson is a writer, artist, and ordained minister in the United Methodist Church. She serves as director of The Wellspring Studio, LLC. Her other books include *Circle of Grace*, *The Cure for Sorrow*, and *Sparrow*. You can find her distinctive writing and artwork at janrichardson.com.